Interrogate Wel

James E Blanchette

Copyright James Blanchette 2014

Published by Spangaloo

Spangaloo Edition

http://spangaloo.com

Standard Copyright eBooks are strictly protected works. You must not perform any actions, including copying, printing and distribution without the author's written or printed consent (the author may have already granted certain terms in a statement within a book.) Some of our eBooks are cleared for personal printing if this option has been enabled, The unauthorized sale of Copyright works in any form is illegal.

Names and companies are used for refer3nce purposes only and are not intended to be an endorsement

Cover Design: Spangaloo

Ebook Formatting : Spangaloo

http://spangaloo.com

Forward:

With the advent of the modern age we find ourselves continuously surrounded by things we don't understand but are still willing to use. The Internet, has been around far longer than most people suspect it has. It did not magically appear in the 1980s, the predates that by a decade or so.

Modern life, is currently filled with all aspects of a connected world. You now find, that you or your business requires a web presence. This may include a website. This book will show you the correct procedures to acquiring the necessary web designer. The correct questions to ask, the answers you need to be looking for. All steps will be explored so that you can make informed decisions and weed out, the web designers that are just out to take your money.

Dr. James Blanchette has been around the computer industry since the very beginning and could be referred to as one of the original geeks. His programming skills extend to 22 different programming languages. He is also worked as a hardware technician for some of the largest companies in the world. He has also acted as the Head Programmer on many large scale web developments.

Independent Technical Services

http://itechecom.com

Contents

Other Books in this Series

The Jargon:

Various terms that are used by web designers are more often than not merely an attempt to confuse the client in the same respect as using big words that nobody understands because it makes them sound more intelligent.

There are probably thousands of words used to describe various aspects of the Internet, web design, hosting and a variety of other aspects dealing with those particulars.

SEO

Organic traffic

Longtail keywords

Keywords

Template design

Marketing analysis

Niche marketing

Programming

They are just a few of the words that get tossed out at you to make it sound like they know what they're talking about, especially if you don't know what they mean. We're now going to break down some of these terms into easy to understand concepts.

SEO

This is an acronym and it simply means, search engine optimization. What this is in reference to, is Google. Google has set itself apart in the online search for information that is surpassed everyone else in the business. They continuously change their algorithms to enhance search results in an attempt to give the client the best possible answer. This is a necessary part of any website design because you can build a fantastic website but if nobody sees it, it has no value.

Most website designers now will tell you that the SEO is included in their designs but failed to mention how they're going to accomplish that. Later in the book, will go to the exact strategies, to determine, if your website designer has the necessary skills, to do as promised.

Organic traffic.

This might sound like something you grow on a farm and nothing to do with a website. The reality is simple. Organic traffic refers to, in most cases, traffic that you get for free from the search engines because of the keywords you selected and used. Nobody can guarantee you how much traffic that is to generate. If you have very finely tuned search engine optimization, then you will definitely increase the traffic to your site.

Longtail keywords and Keywords

To understand longtail keywords, you have to understand the usage of keywords to start with. A keyword is simply a search term. An example of that, is if you type in a single word, at Google and search for it. Let's say "TWITTER" is the chosen word. This will immediately produce a list at Google of relevant terms and websites that use the term TWITTER. Now this will produce millions of results and not really useful if you're looking for something more specific than that. Longtail keywords are designed for how people actually ask questions or search for something. An example of the longtail keyword is something like this. "Cheap red designer shoes in Brisbane." This will produce far fewer results but is more likely to give you the answers you're looking for. Search engine optimization works the best with longtail keywords. Once again, reality is that no one can guarantee you the first page of Google, unless you're searching for a very specific longtail keyword that you've incorporated into your site design and content.

Template design.

Some web designers, will offer you, a variety of different designs for your website. So what this is in reference to, is the designs themselves, how a website looks, and it has nothing to do with how the website operates. It is simply the graphics and layout for your content and images on your site. Now there is a vast difference between custom programming and using canned software like WordPress. WordPress itself only takes a maximum of two hours to set up and get ready for content. There are 100,000 free templates or themes available.

We have run across multiple web designers that charge a lot of money to install a WordPress site. They will attempt to convince you of the value of what they're offering by either (A) not informing you that it is a WordPress site or (B) tell you all the extras and features of their including to make it seem more valuable as a service, i.e. SEO.

Marketing analysis.

Fancy fancy and it really sounds like they're giving you something of value. Marketing analysis is based on an existing business, whether that business is on the web or is land-based. This is research done on the product line or service that is being provided against what is already out there. This is something you should have done before you started the business or website, to see whether you will fit and make money from it. The key rule is that market analysis is designed for something that already exists.

This is not to be confused with another term that is similar, which is called market testing. Once again, equivalent rules apply. What you are, in essence, are doing is testing the market for particular product or service and changing various aspects of the promotion to see the differences.

Most website designers are incapable of either.

Niche marketing.

This refers to a small market for an idea service or product that is only sellable to a select type of client. Once again, if you reference the above paragraphs, this is something you should have done before you decided to build a website.

Niche markets can be extremely profitable; however, a lot of research is necessary to see if you can make money from them and how you can set your product or service apart from the existing competition.

Programming.

This is a very loose term because it references a variety of different aspects when you're dealing with website design. For a website to be able to display on somebody's computer, programming code is necessary. I will not attempt to add confusion with some of the terms used when discussing programming, however, the following widely used. HTML, PHP, Ajax, JavaScript and CSS are the most common programming used on websites. Each one has a different style of application which when used correctly together allow for dynamic websites. What we mean by dynamic websites, our websites that rely on database and other factors to install content to the page. It is not necessary for you to know how to do any of these, while discussing matters with your web designer. It is, however, of the most importance, that your web designer understands these. I'll give you a brief breakdown of what each one is.

HTML is the core language that the World Wide Web runs on and thus your website. Whether or not you have your website programmed in pure PHP or not, at some point it becomes HTML. This is merely a text file that is sent to your browser and then your browser interprets all the references and displays a page. Each item on the page is referenced in some way so if you have an image that needs to be displayed, the reference for the image is included in the text file that your browser receives but not the image itself. Your browser will request the image separately as well as any other elements on the page that need to be displayed.

PHP is a way to preprocess on the server-side before the text file is created that is sent to your browser. The most important aspect of PHP is allowing access to the database where a lot of your information may be contained. It then inserts that information directly into the text file.

AJAX is a combination of programming technologies that allow an even more dynamic web page experience by including things that happen on the client side. A simple example of Ajax, is when you're on twitter, and you click the follow button. You do not reload the entire page again, but the button changes color and you how are following that particular individual. This is Ajax at its finest using a callback routine that involves several programming aspects to allow that to happen. Ajax is also the easiest of everything to break and cause unpredictable results.

JAVASCRIPT has been around for quite a while, originally created by Sun technologies as a scripting language to add a dynamic impact on the client side. Ajax utilizes many aspects of JavaScript to performance functions. Simply stated, JavaScript tends to add the bells and whistles to your website.

CSS is responsible for layout aspects of your website. It's what produces the colors, some of the graphics and the look and feel of the website. This allows you to control fonts, colors, hovering effects and much more. CSS has been standardized. However, not all browsers interpreted quite the same way, and you must use care when developing a website that things will display as closely as possible in all browsers.

Please note that browser interpretation varies widely, and it is almost impossible to have a web page display in all browsers the same way. There will be small aspects that have changed. Other browsers like IE 6, IE 7, IE 8, IE 9 do not respond well to the latest versions of CSS, which available as version 3.

It is not that important you understand fully what all these programming types are and exactly how they function, the above, is just to give you a rough understanding of those technologies. Information abounds, all over the web that will allow you to learn to use these yourself, but bear in mind, there is a learning curve involved.

Don't be confused by your web designer, who throws of terms that you that you don't understand. Google is readily available to look up information on any aspect of web design that he or she is talking about. When in doubt, look it up.

Decide First

This is probably the most important chapter because, it is the starting point. If you don't know what you want, getting it is going to be more difficult. You need a clearly laid-out plan of what you want your website to do.

Do you want it to make money?

Do you want to provide information?

Do you want to generate leads for your business?

These are just a couple of questions, that you need to ask yourself even before you start looking for a web designer. There are fundamental ways to accomplish any type of web design, and it is important that you know what the final outcome needs to be.

These are questions, that your web designer, if they are any good, will have to ask you to determine the type of site and designs that you're going to require. The more information that they can get from you, the easier it will be a map of a strategy and design your website.

If your web designer doesn't ask you any questions, hang up the phone and find somebody else, it is really that simple.

Now I'm not saying that you have to have all the answers upfront, but you at least have to be having a direction to go in. Site colors, fonts, images and relevant content will need to be decided upon, long before your site goes live.

You need to decide, if you are responsible for adding content to your site after it's complete or if it will be the web designer.

Depending upon your needs, WordPress sites are the easiest to set up, maintain and add content to, but they are not for all types of websites. Sometimes, depending upon your needs, a custom programmed website is your only real solution. The downside, is that often, the website is not set up, to allow you to make changes and now requires the use of the original web designer and or programmer. If not correctly negotiated, this can be come a money pit. For a lot of individuals, this will not be an option.

That is where a clear plan comes into play. If you know exactly what you want and what you want your website to do, you can decide on the correct course of action.

For my company, we do a lot of custom programming because of our specific client needs. We do not however, build websites, that require constant maintenance from us. We generally build in an admin menu, that allows a client to make most alterations to not only content but also layout. Most people think this is a bad business model on our part because essentially, we have programmed ourselves out of a job. What they are referring to is a constant source of income that is coming from a website that needs maintenance on a continuous basis. That is where they make the most money. We provide a website to a client that is easy for them to make changes to so that we don't have to constanly maintain it for them. This makes our clients happy and because of our business model are more likely to use our services again in the future.

Once again, I have to reiterate, decide first, then build.

An example is this. You want to market an e-book or similar products along those lines. You probably don't require a custom website. The reasons for this are simple. You have one or two products that you want to display and give people the opportunity to buy. You can use off-site companies to do this for you, companies like Amazon, Smashwords, Barnes & Noble and kobo. You don't have to worry about distribution, collecting payments or anything else. Your only job at this point is to drive traffic to those sites where your book is available.

WordPress is ideally suited to this type of site. So now, your task is to write articles that surround the book that you're offering. Through the articles, if well written, will produce the necessary search engine optimization to drive traffic to your site for people to look at what you're offering.

Next example, is a bit more complicated. You own a restaurant and of course, you want people to show up and eat there. How can you make this happen?

Once again, that would depend on your budget. Is it a small restaurant? Is it a large restaurant? Do you take reservations? Do you want to offer coupons and discounts to people on your mailing list?

These are just a couple of the questions that need to be answered before you make any decisions. If you have a small restaurant, then WordPress is probably the correct way to go and a lot of your content that will be displayed on your WordPress site will be about food as well is what you're offering.

A very large restaurant, that seats 50 to 100 people and reservations are necessary, then you're probably looking at custom programming. It, nonetheless, does not have to be extensive and you possibly only still need a five-page site. There are elements that need to be addressed. You need a way to create the mailing list and then also send out to that mailing list. For on-line reservations, you need a couple of things. You need a way for your clients to do the booking on-line as well as an admin menu that allows your staff to process the bookings.

Everything depends on what you want your website to be able to do but that does not mean you should have to pay outrageous prices to get what you want. If your web designer or web developer, is worth anything, he, she or they will walk you through all the necessary steps and ask you all the right questions so that everybody's moving forward, and the site becomes complete.

Web Designer Questions

This is a list of questions to ask your web designer, but they are in no particular order, mostly because you need to ask all of them.

1). Where are you located?

This might even sound like a silly question, however, it can be extremely relevant because it has bearing on how easy it will be to get in contact with your web designer. Is he in the same country? Is he in the same city?

Even if they are in the same country, some countries are large, and you have to determine time zones. Are they awake while I'm asleep? Some people like to outsource their design work to India or the Philippines and that can be a good option, but it contains its own risks.

2). How can I contact you?

Contact is the single most important aspect when dealing with somebody who is designing your website. If you can't contact them, how are you going to communicate the changes that need to be done? There are many aspects to communication, email, Skype and phone calls are probably about the easiest. Your web designer should give you multiple ways to contact them.

3). Do they speak your language?

Sounds like a moot point, however, it is not. If you outsource your web design work to a foreign country, you have to determine if they are truly understanding your or not. Often times, communication becomes a stumbling block where neither party genuinely understands the needs of the other.

4). Do you have references?

References are necessary, and they can come in many forms. Ideally, it is more than just showing you a couple of websites that they may or may not have designed. Ask for e addresses to some of their clients that will tell you what their experience with them was like. Perhaps phone numbers, so you can call. When you look at a website, you can't see any coding behind it, all you can see how it kind of works and what it looks like.

Being able to contact people that they've done work for in the past, is a necessary ingredient for building trust.

5). Who owns the code?

The in and out of who owns the code, will be discussed in detail in a later chapter. This is still a very relevant question, and your web designer should be able to easily answer it. The short answer is that you want, to own all the coding for the site. However, this isn't always possible for a lot of different reasons.

6). How long is it going to take?

Web site development completion times can vary depending upon the amount of work that actually needs to be done. Now, first off, you've already given the web designer everything they need to work with when it comes to the ideas and how you want the site to look like, to be like and any other pertinent details that are required. Once you come to an understanding of what is needed, this question becomes relevant. For a simple five-page site, completion time should not take any longer than a month. I fact, it should be sooner than that. That also depends on the complexity because it may indeed take longer. What you're looking for are from the web designer is a general time frame because sub web designers can do it faster than others, and everything may depend upon their particular workload. If you've chosen a large company to build your website and is not a lot of money involved, it may not have any priority.

7). What is it going to cost?

The web designer should be able to give you some, at least a ballpark figure work with. Now you can use this, to compare rates, with other companies. Make sure, when you're comparing rates, that you're comparing the same types of services that are going to be provided.

8). What is included in the price?

You're looking for a fairly comprehensive list of what they are offering. If they are vague, walk away.

9). What are the payment arrangements?

Structured payments are the only type of payment you should accept. Normally, most web designers will require a deposit of some sort, and that's perfectly acceptable. What is not allowable is paying the entire amount, up front. If you pay all the money, they lack the incentive to finish it, or finish it within the timeframe specified.

To avoid this, I suggest, breaking down your payments into four equal payments that are payable at various stages of project completion. This is how we do it, and it seems to work well for all of our clients.

As for amounts, we would not suggest you pay any more than 25% as an initial down payment.

10). Where will the website be hosted while it's being built?

This is a difficult one because you do not want your website to be accessible to the world in an unfinished state. Most good web designers will give you various options to choose from. The preferred, that the website is built on their servers, commonly as a subdomain of their server. Google has limited or no access to the subdomains without somebody providing a link to it, so there's little or no danger of Google getting the wrong impression of you before you're ready. As well, it easy to suggest changes, go over details and perfect the website before it goes live.

These represent the top 10 questions you need to ask your web designer before you agree on a contract. Do not limit yourself to these questions alone. Any questions or concerns that you happen to have, should be spoken about during the initial discussions.

Basic SEO

This section is not intended to be an exhaustive tutorial on SEO but rather, to give you a basic understanding of how it all tends to work.

Google recommends the following to get better rankings in their search engine:

Make pages primarily for users, not for search engines. Don't deceive your users or present different content to search engines than you display to users, which is commonly referred to as cloaking.

Make a site with a clear hierarchy and text links. Every page should be reachable from at least one static text link.

Create a useful, information rich site, and write pages that clearly and accurately describe your content. Make sure that your <title> elements and ALT attributes are descriptive and accurate.

Keep the links on a given page to a reasonable number (fewer than 100).

What that really means is that Google wants you to present your site in a clear and orderly manner that is designed around the users that may visit your site. You need to make all the content on your site understandable and readable. Google frowns on sites that attempt to circumvent the algorithms that are designed to collect the information. Various methods have been devised to trick Google, unfortunately for those attempting, Google has a tendency to figure out the deceptions really quick.

SEO itself can be accomplished rather easily, but it is something that needs to be tweaked on a regular basis. From a programming viewpoint, Google looks at the headlines for your site, titles, subtitles and then finally content. For the keywords you're using, if you overuse the keyword, it will actually detract from your rating at Google instead of increasing it's like you thought it was going to do.

An example of SEO is something like this.

The title of the article on your site is, "Golf lessons for beginners."

Because this is a title, Google now looks forward to finding an article that is about golf lessons for beginners. In the article, you should also have subheadings that are relevant to the article and/or keywords that you want to use, without overusing keywords.

In the content itself, you should also try to include the keywords from the title as well as being able to include them in the order that they appear because this will produce a longtail keyword. When someone searches for the longtail keyword, your site may come up near the top of the Google search.

Most people tend to overdo it and as a result hurt their rankings instead of improving them. You can't simply mention golf lesson's beginners continuously through the article because it is not consistent with normal conversation or writing. If it doesn't read right Google will notice. As well, you need to have your article free of spelling mistakes as well as grammatical error, or you will be penalized.

The next point is perhaps the most valid of all; Google is looking for original content, not something you copied and pasted from somewhere else.

That is the bare basics of how SEO works, but we will explain more.

No I know I mention articles, but this applies to all websites, the content on the page matters. The titles matter; the links matter, basically everything means something.

Example.

Your business is Joe's plumbing and guess what, you offer plumbing services. You now want to make your site more search engines friendly as well as providing information and gathering leads so that you get some work out of it, which is the main goal of your website. How are you going to do that? What is going to set you apart from the competition? Is your website easy to navigate?

For Joe, here are some of the things we like to recommend.

The phone number must be predominantly displayed on the website, as well as the address. Perhaps the phone number should be listed a few times on the page.

Joe has a simple website, really only two pages, the main page and a contact page.

This is insufficient; Google seems to require more than that. They want a privacy policy page, terms of use page, a contact page and in most cases, an about us page. All of these pages need to be built because it will help Joe rank higher in the search engines because of the compliance.

Joe's a local business, so he is looking for regional leads and not worldwide leads. He needs to mention his city on the main page. Mentioning his state or province is also quite helpful. That means for the search engines, his city and location should be mentioned at least twice on the page but probably not more than that.

Now we get down to content; Joseph is a Plummer. What can we say about that?

Probably, a lot of things, but we want to do is target a very specific audience, people with plumbing problems or people that are building new houses and need primary pipes installed, hot-water tanks and the simalar installed.

We now have the ability to put several titles on a page that pertain to various aspects of his business. A tag line on the site could read something like; we make your plumbing problems a thing of the past. We have now mentioned a couple of keywords, plumbing and problems. People are searching because they have a problem, and because they need a plumber.

We can't stop there; Joe also installs hot-water tanks, bathtubs, sinks and fixtures, so we need subtitles on the page that reflects this. He has to mention as many of his various services as he can on the page without overcrowding it. If he can use as many possible combination about plumbing on a page then that will produce excellent results but you have to remember it's not just keywords, it's keywords in a particular order that become longtail keywords.

An example of a longtail keyword.

how much is a new hot water tank

hot water tank installation cost

hot water tank installation

(all of the above longtail keywords have a high suggested bid which means they are searched for often)

So with these three examples that are often searched for according to Google, what can we do with them?

Well, we can include that string of words in the content of the site and or a sub heading like this.

Sub Heading

Hot water tank installation

Content under that may read something like.

Our hot water tank installation cost is the lowest in Brisbane and we warranty our workmanship for a full five years. Give us a call right now for a free estimate.

Joe's other services can be handled in much the same way.

BUT Joe, why stop there, if you add a few more pages to your site that also use your chosen keywords in articles, even better results can be obtained.

Joe could write, or have someone else write a few articles on simple plumbing repairs that people can do themselves. Now once again in these articles you want to include as many pertinent keywords about Joe's business as possible, without overdoing it. The upside is that people searching at Google using Joe's keywords, they may find Joe's article pages about a problem they're having and that he's providing a solution for. Joe looks like a good guy and ultimately as he increased his trust level with this potential client, the client will now look at other areas of Joe site to see what else he has to offer.

That is the raw power of search engine optimization. There are so many different ways that you can drive customers to your site that are absolutely free. It actually is a coin name; it is called **Organic Traffic** and it something you can never pay for. It is simply the result of people searching and finding information.

It is beyond the scope of this book to deliver all the in and out of SEO, but it is something that you have to learn and understand how it works.

When your web designer says he's including SEO with your website design, you need and ask him how he's going to do that. You need to ask for the particulars of what is going to be done and what methods he's going to use.

If you do your own keyword searches, including longtail searches that are pertinent to your business, there are many suggestions that you can give him and this will help increase the traffic to your site. If you open up an ad words account at Google, even if you don't purchase advertising from them, you can do keyword searches in the keyword planner.

Who Owns the Code?

Owning the code is very tricky thing. Mostly, it is determined by where the code originates. Most often than not, what you truly own on the website is merely the content.

Here is why.

If you use WordPress, that particular software package is handled under a GPL license which gives you the right to use and modify the code as you see fit but does not give you ownership or the copyright to it.

In custom coding, it depends on what the developer or designer or programmer is offering. They may have a bunch of code routines that are also handled under the GPL license or the Commons license which means they don't own them either but are just using them. When it comes to the actual code that's been written they may give it to you as part of the website design or may withhold parts of it.

Withholding parts of the code is common because these are routines and functions that the particular program or designer uses all the time. An example of that is that we have an image manipulation function that we have written and because of the number of hours, perfecting that function we want to be able to reuse it. If we sell a website design with that function in it and include all rights to it, we can not use it again. We would have to develop a brand-new routine that has to be completely rewritten to remain different from the one that was sold. What we do in this case, is provide a one-off license to use the code generally at no charge but with the understanding that they can't transfer that code anybody else without permission. That does not mean they can't sell the website to some else and use it intact, it just can't be used on any other website without permission.

When we write code, generally anything that pertains directly to the website is included in part of the package.

You need to ask your web developer or web designer what you're getting and what you do own at the end of it. You may indeed be surprised by the answer. Once again, the caveat here is, if they are vague about who will end up owning the code that makes your website run, walk away.

It is generally necessary to put everything in writing so that both parties know exactly what the particulars are for the transactions, and rights are. It doesn't have to be a long, legalese contract, but it has to encompass all the details that are necessary. Failing to put things in writing could come back to haunt you. You may find that suddenly, that you do not own any rights the website whatsoever, and your web developer sells it out from under you. Make sure that your own the domain name and as many rights to the code as you can possibly get.

Web Hosting-what you need.

Web hosting for your site is available everywhere. It's not created equal and you, have to determine what level of service you require for your website. How much traffic are you going to get, how much bandwidth you use, how many databases and many other details.

Another pertinent question is, is your web designer also providing hosting. If that's the case, then what is the cost and what are you getting for the cost.

Hosting costs vary, a low price could be a great thing or a horrible mistake. Go Daddy offers hosting along with domain name registration. If you set up a website on Go Daddy that is a WordPress site (they make it super easy to install), moving to another host provider is a difficult thing. The number of problems you will get can be overwhelming. You have issues with your themes that you can't change certain aspects of your themes now because they originated on Go Daddy and although the site still works if you have someone semi-competent enough to transfer it, making changes is more difficult. The cost of hosting on Go Daddy is very cheap but has imposed limitations that often times are hard to determine. One of the great drawbacks with hosting there is email. They limit how many emails you can send in a given day, and if you require more they want you to apply for it. They have an opportunity at this point to turn you down and tell you you can't have the increase.

That is unacceptable if your business or you are selling anything. Other major hosting companies include companies such as HOSTgator. Wellwithin the same price ranges Go Daddy, once again hidden limitations.

What you need for hosting is a hosting company that will provide you with a full cPanel. CPanel itself is an add-on built into the hosting server that allows easy access to everything about your server or virtual server. If you're hosting website anywhere, is a virtual server, and it simply means that you have a piece of the server at your disposal.

CPanel makes it easy to move an entire website to a different server as long as his running cPanel. It also gives you better backup options and a whole list of stats that may pertain to you in different ways. All this is available only on web hosting companies that provide you with that. We also offer hosting and of course, we offer cPanel as part of every hosting package that we have.

It doesn't stop there; you have to determine what you really need, how much traffic and how many system resources you will require to determine the correct type of hosting that is involved. If you have a few million visitors a year, your best choice is going to be your very own dedicated server because you are consuming resources and most hosting companies at that point will start throttling you to stop using all the resources that were supposed be shared amongst everyone.

The odds are you don't need your own server yet but you still looking for hosting and it has to be at a reasonable price for what you're getting.

This is the bare list that you want for a small business or website.

Storage space: at least a gig.

Databases: at least one.

Bandwidth: at least five gigs.

Email accounts: at least three.

CPanel: as mentioned above.

Access: as many ways as possible but at least FTP, WebDav so you can upload files. Microsoft expressions and other software packages that help you write the code for websites can and will utilize either the two above.

Arranging Payments.

Payment arrangements have to be negotiated and cannot be inflexible.

The number-one rule, should be the only rule, you have to be comfortable with the payment structure.

Do not allow a web designer the hard sell you into something that you don't want and don't need. They want to lock you in and have you sign on the dotted line, but if you're unsure, then you need time to think about it. Take the time.

Payment structure should be reasonable to both parties. A down payment of over 25% is unwarranted in almost every case. A down payment of 100% is ridiculous, and you need to walk away from it.

We tend to structure payments into four easily divisible payments of the total. However, we will work with our client's to ensure that payment arrangements are acceptable to them, even if we have to split it into six, seven or more payments.

Payment should be made it acceptable stages of work, not a timeframe. Once a site is 50% complete, that's how much work has been done to it, and if they are inside their timeframe that it becomes an acceptable payment if you've arranged to pay the at that point of completion.

I can't stress this enough, insist that you pay at completion points and not at a timed interval. The reason for that is quite simple; they haven't done anything for the last month on your website and still want to payment because you've agreed to pay them monthly. They have no incentive to finish your site to get paid because eventually, they get all the money any ways whether it is complete or not. That is an unacceptable payment arrangement.

Making payments at completion points that are visible to you, so that you can see where the progress really is at, is the only way to go, and if they're unwilling to make these kinds of arrangements, then perhaps he should be looking for somebody else long before you sign on the dotted line.

When you find a good web designer, they will be willing to work with you every step of the way and keep you informed.

There will also seek your approval in various stages, including simple things like colors and fonts.

Whether or not the images that they are using are acceptable to you.

Whether or not you like the menuing system.

Their main focus should be a happy customer because a happy customer will recommend them to their friends. Customer service is the name of the game, and you have to remember that one simple thing.

They want your business. To get your business, they have to prove that there were worthy of it. They have to build the trust and be reliable.

Another part of payments, doesn't really deal with payments. It deals with warranties. How long after your website is complete will they continue to work on it if there are problems.

To date, there is not a software package in the world, that is error-free. Problems crop up in the strangest ways, and you require a web designer that can go in and fix whatever the problem is, if it is a result of their code.

Bear this in mind, if you did something to break it, they are well within their rights to bill you for the event.

Web Design Concepts

One of the most important aspects of website design is what does the website look like.

How functional is it?

Is easy to navigate?

Is the content easy to read and understand?

Are the graphics too big it or overpowering?

Is the website design balanced?

All the above questions are valid. The correct website design makes a website accomplish its goals. If you are Joe the plumber, you want people to call you because that is the main purpose of his site. Other sites have different purposes and that always depend on what exactly you are trying to accomplish.

Let's go into detail about makes a good website design.

Many people have huge flash presentations as a lead-in to the website and while they look great, they do absolutely nothing to further what you created a website for. Most often than not Google ignores the page because it doesn't really contain anything that's relevant. Google knows there is a flash file there but does not process it. The second concern of course is how long the flash presentation takes the load. Your site must load fast, the faster the better. Flash presentations, therefore, not really recommended and or to be used sparingly.

Your website must contain at least five pages.

The front page.

A contact page.

A policy page.

A terms of use page.

An about us page.

Each one of these pages has a purpose and most deal with credibility with Google. Without these pages, you will not be listed as an authority on any subject as well they won't look at you as a real business.

The front page.

Starting with the front page, you need a menu system that is clear and easy to use. You need titles in areas on the page for displaying different things. You need a main area on the page that presents the outstanding idea of the website.

Another concept, originally started by newspapers, is called above the fold. In newspapers, they were folded in half. On the front page of the newspaper was always the large headline, and the most important stories were located on the top half of the paper. Google now is capable of knowing what is on the top part of your website, the part that shows without you having to scroll further down. You want your most important concepts, titles and content to be easily visible in that top section.

HTML contains tags which your browser uses to change how things are displayed. These are called the H tags which refer to header tags and in the code itself. It will look something like this.

<H1> An awesome headline about My site </H1>

Everything between those tags will be displayed in the largest font possible. Typically, there are 6 H tags and those reflect the different sizing, one through six. One being the largest and six being the smallest. These are title tags and subheading tags that Google very specifically looks for in articles and content listed on your front page. It is very important that your web designer gets this right.

When it comes to images, you want the images to be viewable, but you do not want them to take up the entire top of the page.

There's much more on the front page that needs to be there, but it depends on what type of website you actually have and what you're trying to sell or present. The front page your website being the very first thing anybody sees when they visit your website is the most important page on the site. Make sure, with your web designer that you get this absolutely right.

As discussed earlier, basic contact information is necessary above the fold depending on what you're trying to do. If you want somebody to call, make it easy for them to find the number, put it at the top. Pertinent contact details will depend upon what your exact purpose of the website is, but let's say you have a newsletter that you want in the sign up for. If they don't easily find where to sign up, they never will. You need the page to be as simple as possible to get what you need done in front of the user. There must be a call to action on the page, something you want them to do.

Other sites, exist purely for making money directly from advertising. We've seen some sites that are absolutely ghastly, so crowded with ads that you can't find any content on the page and this becomes unquestionably and people leave. Each page should have a clear directive that you want to present if you have a multiple page website with lots of articles etc. One or two ads on the page, really is the limit and the advertising should match the content of the page.

A quick note on Google's advertising, when someone clicks a Google ad on your page, they leave your site. Very few will ever use the back button, so that person is gone for good. If the intent of your website is just to have them click on a Google ad, then you do not have a problem, and it will work exactly that way. If you want the person to stay on your site, select advertisers who will have the ad open up in a new page or new window. You've worked really hard, to get the person to this front page your site; your only real job now is to keep them there.

The contact page.

This is a very important page, and it should come with a whole list of rules. You don't want spam, but you want your contact page to be easy for somebody to get a hold of you. Never allow the mailto routines to be used. Most spammers collect email addresses this way. It is better to use a self-contained routine that the spammer has no access to, to send mail to you. Any even vaguely competent programmer or web designer can do this.

The information on the contact page should be relevant to your situation. If your land-based business then some of the information on that page should reflect your hours of operation, phone numbers and addresses as well as being able to contact you by email.

The privacy page and Terms of Use.

Websites collect information, information that is used in a variety of different ways, whether be cookies or sessions. Your privacy policy must clearly reflect how you use this data. This also concerns email because email spam rules are changing worldwide. It's not enough just to collect someones email address; you must give them a way to opt out, as well as a way to initially prove that they want to be on your list. This is called the double opt in method.

Everything about your privacy page is important and Google looks at it, without the privacy page you will never get a good ranking in Google.

There are many examples of privacy pages as well as websites that will produce privacy pages for you. In WordPress there are many plug-ins that will produce not only the privacy page but the terms of use page after you answering just a couple of questions.

The terms of use is also absolutely necessary because it lays down the legalities of someone using your website. These can be long complicated boring documents, most often most people don't even bother to read them, but Google does, so make sure these pages are included by the web designer.

The about us page.

While not totally necessary for Google yet, is a good idea to always have this particular page. It helps build trust because you give information about you and your company. In most people's eyes this makes you more credible. This page does not have to be long and complicated but is always good to share any information your comfortable sharing.

Putting it all together.

Your website needs to strive for the correct balance between functionality and content. You need the SEO built-in from the start without having to try to retrofitted later. If you do this, it makes it so much easier.

Google analytics has been around for quite a while, and it is necessary that you set it up so it is used on your site. This will give you a wealth of information that you can now use to fine tune and tweak your site. If the keywords in the longtail keywords are not quite right, Google analytics can probably point you in the right direction. They list all the keywords people are using to find your site, and that allows you to fine-tune the SEO.

Once again, this is something that you have to work out with your web designer so that changes can be easily done, and preferably you get to do them yourself. Finding what works and what doesn't work is a trial and error in almost every case. Nobody produces a website that is perfect and instantly attracts users. It is a long hard road and it takes work and is always it is up to you to decide how much work is needed and what needs to be done.

This section is not an exhaustive study of web design because all the aspects of web design become a massive field of study. We tried to keep the concepts readable and easy to understand. Nobody's asking you become an expert. However, when dealing with the web designer, been as knowledgeable as possible is the best course. Google itself will provide you many answers that you're seeking with the questions you still have.

Other books in this series.

Interrogate SEO.

Much more in depth study of the ins and outs of

SEO.

Interrogate Traffic.

Traffic and how to get it.

Interrogate Web Hosting.

Everything about web hosting and servers.

Glossary of Terms:

Algorithm

In mathematics and computer science, an algorithm is a step-by-step procedure for calculations. Algorithms are used for calculation, data processing, and automated reasoning.

An algorithm is an effective method expressed as a finite list of well-defined instructions for calculating a function. Starting from an initial state and initial input (perhaps empty), the instructions describe a computation that, when executed, proceeds through a finite number of well-defined successive states, eventually producing "output" and terminating at a final ending state. The transition from one state to the next is not necessarily deterministic; some algorithms, known as randomized algorithms, incorporate random input.

AJAX

An acronym for Asynchronous JavaScript and XML) is a group of interrelated Web development techniques used on the client-side to create asynchronous Web applications. With Ajax, Web applications can send data to, and retrieve data from, a server asynchronously (in the background) without interfering with the display and behavior of the existing page. Data can be retrieved using the XMLHttpRequest object. Despite the name, the use of XML is not required; JSON is often used instead (see AJAJ), and the requests do not need to be asynchronous.

Ajax is not a single technology, but a group of technologies. HTML and CSS can be used in combination to mark up and style information. The DOM is accessed with JavaScript to dynamically display - and allow the user to interact with - the information presented. JavaScript and the XMLHttpRequest object provide a method for exchanging data asynchronously between browser and server to avoid full page reloads.

AJAJ

Stands for Asynchronous JavaScript and JSON. AJAJ is used primarily with server communication. Unlike its predecessor AJAX which uses XML, in AJAJ the content sent back and forth between the client and server is strictly JSON. The term AJAJ has been used since at least 2006. Despite being a more precise term, use of the term AJAJ did not become widespread, and as such many people describe a process as "AJAX" when they are in fact talking about AJAJ (because they are receiving JSON formatted data in the response, not XML).

PHP

Is a server-side scripting language designed for web development but also used as a general-purpose programming language. As of January 2013, PHP was installed on more than 240 million websites (39% of those sampled) and 2.1 million web servers. Originally created by Rasmus Lerdorf in 1994, the reference implementation of PHP (the Zend Engine) is now produced by The PHP Group. While PHP originally stood for Personal Home Page, it now stands for PHP: Hypertext Preprocessor.

PHP code can be simply mixed with HTML code, or it can be used in combination with various templating engines and web frameworks. PHP code is usually processed by a PHP interpreter, which is usually implemented as a web server's native module or a Common Gateway Interface (CGI) executable. After the PHP code is interpreted and executed, the web server sends resulting output to its client, usually in form of a part of the generated web page – for example, PHP code can generate a web page's HTML code, an image, or some other data. PHP has also evolved to include a command-line interface (CLI) capability and can be used in standalone graphical applications.

PHP is free software released under the PHP License. PHP has been widely ported and can be deployed on most web servers on almost every operating system and platform, free of charge

HTML or HyperText Markup Language

Is the standard markup language used to create web pages.

HTML is written in the form of HTML elements consisting of tags enclosed in angle brackets (like <html>). HTML tags most commonly come in pairs like <h1> and </h1>, although some tags represent empty elements and so are unpaired, for example <img>. The first tag in a pair is the start tag, and the second tag is the end tag (they are also called opening tags and closing tags).

The purpose of a web browser is to read HTML documents and compose them into visible or audible web pages. The browser does not display the HTML tags, but uses the tags to interpret the content of the page. HTML describes the structure of a website semantically along with cues for presentation, making it a markup language rather than a programming language.

HTML elements form the building blocks of all websites. HTML allows images and objects to be embedded and can be used to create interactive forms. It provides a means to create structured documents by denoting structural semantics for text such as headings, paragraphs, lists, links, quotes and other items. It can embed scripts written in languages such as JavaScript which affect the behavior of HTML web pages.

Web browsers can also refer to Cascading Style Sheets (CSS) to define the look and layout of text and other material. The W3C, maintainer of both the HTML and the CSS standards, encourages the use of CSS over explicit presentational HTML.

Cascading Style Sheets (CSS)

Is a style sheet language used for describing the look and formatting of a document written in a markup language. While most often used to style web pages and interfaces written in HTML and XHTML, the language can be applied to any kind of XML document, including plain XML, SVG and XUL. CSS is a cornerstone specification of the web and almost all web pages use CSS style sheets to describe their presentation.

CSS is designed primarily to enable the separation of document content from document presentation, including elements such as the layout, colors, and fonts. This separation can improve content accessibility, provide more flexibility and control in the specification of presentation characteristics, enable multiple pages to share formatting, and reduce complexity and repetition in the structural content (such as by allowing for tableless web design).

CSS can also allow the same markup page to be presented in different styles for different rendering methods, such as on-screen, in print, by voice (when read out by a speech-based browser or screen reader) and on Braille-based, tactile devices. It can also be used to allow the web page to display differently depending on the screen size or device on which it is being viewed. While the author of a document typically links that document to a CSS file, readers can use a different style sheet, perhaps one on their own computer, to override the one the author has specified. However if the author or the reader did not link the document to a specific style sheet the default style of the browser will be applied.

CSS specifies a priority scheme to determine which style rules apply if more than one rule matches against a particular element. In this so-called cascade, priorities or weights are calculated and assigned to rules, so that the results are predictable.

JavaScript (JS)

Not to be confused with Java (programming language), Java (software platform), or Javanese script.

Is a dynamic computer programming language. It is most commonly used as part of web browsers, whose implementations allow client-side scripts to interact with the user, control the browser, communicate asynchronously, and alter the document content that is displayed. It is also being used in server-side network programming (with Node.js), game development and the creation of desktop and mobile applications.

JavaScript is a prototype-based scripting language with dynamic typing and has first-class functions. Its syntax was influenced by C. JavaScript copies many names and naming conventions from Java, but the two languages are otherwise unrelated and have very different semantics. The key design principles within JavaScript are taken from the Self and Scheme programming languages. It is a multi-paradigm language, supporting object-oriented, imperative, and functional programming styles.

The application of JavaScript in use outside of web pages — for example, in PDF documents, site-specific browsers, and desktop widgets — is also significant. Newer and faster JavaScript VMs and platforms built upon them (notably Node.js) have also increased the popularity of JavaScript for server-side web applications. On the client side, JavaScript was traditionally implemented as an interpreted language but just-in-time compilation is now performed by recent (post-2012) browsers.

JavaScript was formalized in the ECMAScript language standard and is primarily used as part of a web browser (client-side JavaScript). This enables programmatic access to objects within a host environment.

Search engine optimization (SEO)

is the process of affecting the visibility of a website or a web page in a search engine's "natural" or un-paid ("organic") search results. In general, the earlier (or higher ranked on the search results page), and more frequently a site appears in the search results list, the more visitors it will receive from the search engine's users. SEO may target different kinds of search, including image search, local search, video search, academic search, news search and industry-specific vertical search engines.

As an Internet marketing strategy, SEO considers how search engines work, what people search for, the actual search terms or keywords typed into search engines and which search engines are preferred by their targeted audience. Optimizing a website may involve editing its content, HTML and associated coding to both increase its relevance to specific keywords and to remove barriers to the indexing activities of search engines. Promoting a site to increase the number of backlinks, or inbound links, is another SEO tactic.

www.ingramcontent.com/pod-product-compliance
Lightning Source LLC
Chambersburg PA
CBHW051212050326
40689CB00008B/1282